KB244203

The Myths in the Stars

About Wise & Wide

- A systematic 6-level English reading program based on Lexile® measures
- Diverse and interesting topics chosen from the elementary curriculums of Korea and English speaking western countries
- Well-written books in various forms including fiction stories, descriptive texts, and classics retold
- The informative but original fiction stories grab your interest, leading to the easy and clear understanding of the educational content.
- Improve thinking skills with solid after-reading activities at all levels of the series.

Wise & Wide is a 6-level English reading program that consists of 60 books and each level is systematically divided by Lexile® measures. The Lexile® Framework for Reading is the most popular reading measuring system in American formal education curriculums and many English programs. Over 20 out of 50 states in the U.S. mark Lexile® measures directly on students' final report cards and over 300 well-known publishers adopt and use Lexile® measures.

Experience many kinds of readings written by professional writers from the U.S. and England. They used interesting topics that were carefully chosen after analyzing elementary curriculums from around the world including Korea, the U.S., England, and Australia among many others. Comprehensive after-reading activities including graphic organizers, speaking tasks, and After-reading Tests are ready for you.

Levels in the series and their corresponding Lexile® measures

Level	Lexile® measures	U.S. Grade
Level 1	Below 200L	Pre K - K
Level 2	190L - 400L	Lower Grade 1
Level 3	350L - 530L	Upper Grade 1
Level 4	420L - 650L	Grade 2
Level 5	520L - 940L	Grade 3 - 4
Level 6	830L - 1070L	Grade 5 - 6

* Smart Readers: Wise & Wide level 1 is applicable to the preschool level in the U.S.

* The source of the relationship between Lexile® measures and U.S. school grades: CCSS(Common Core State Standards) FOR ENGLISH LANGUAGE ARTS, APPENDIX A (2012, which is used by 45 states in the U.S.)

Topic List

	Level 1	Level 2	Level 3	Level 4	Level 5	Level 6
Book 1	Science>Biology: The hibernation of animals Story	Science>Biology: Living and nonliving things Story	Science>Biology> Animals & the Environment: Sea otters Story	Environment> Living with nature: The diver & the persimmon tree Story	Science>Biology> Animal: Amazing animals of the Amazon Story	Science>Biology: Germs, transmitted diseases Story
Book 2	Literature> World classics: Aesop's fables Story	Literature> Traditional fairy tale: Old tales about stones Story	Social Studies> Economy: To run a business to make and save money Story	Science>Biology> Plants: Photosynthesis Story	Science>Earth science: Earth's layers,earthquakes, volcanoes, and earth's atmosphere Report	Mathematics> Sequence: The golden ratio & the Fibonacci sequence Story
Book 3	Science>Physics: How shadows are formed Story	Literature> World classics: Peter Pan Story	Science>Scientific technology: Nanobots Story	Literature>Myths: World's creation stories Story	Literature> Legend: The story of King Arthur Story	Literature>Myths: Constellation myths Story
Book 4	Literature> Traditional literature: The Talmud Story	Science>Biology> Animal: Polar bears Story	Science>Biology> Animal: Mountain gorillas Story	Social Studies> Cultural anthropology: Amazing ancient cultures of the world Story	Science> Earth science: Clouds and weather Story	
Book 5	Social Studies> Ethics: Rules in daily life Story	Science>Biology: The five senses Report	Social Studies> Cultural anthropology: Astonishing festivals Report	Art>Music: Stories from two operas Story	Social Studies> World culture & history: The Renaissance Story	
Book 6	Social Studies> World geography & travel: Tourist attractions around the world Story	Science>Biology> Animal: Dinosaurs Story	Science> Astronomy: The solar system Story	Social Studies> People: Three great people who overcame hardships Story	Science>Scientific technology: The wonderful world of robots Report	
Book 7				Science & Social Studies> Technology & culture: Inventions from around the world Report	Art>Works of art: Famous paintings Report	
Book 8						
Book 9						
Book 10						

10 books in each level will be published.

How to Use This Book

• Before Reading

You can easily find the topic and what kind of story you are about to read.

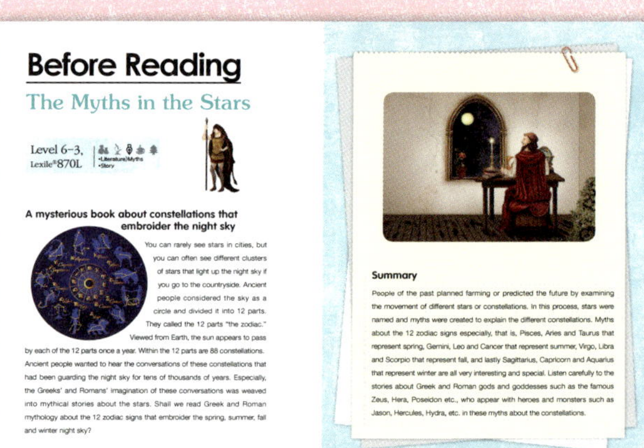

• The text

All the stories were written by professional writers from the U.S. and England, so you will read authentic and appropriate English sentences and expressions in every book in the series.

• Pop Quiz

Check out right away if you understand what you have just read by solving a pop quiz that checks your comprehension.

• Key Words

The key words and expressions on each page are listed for you to easily study them.

• Aha! Tips

Download free Korean explanations at *www.ihappyhouse.co.kr* for all of the sentences marked with "Aha!". These explain cultural, scientific, and economic knowledge or they deal with aspects of English such as grammatical structures or idiomatic expressions. There are lots of "Aha! Tips" to help you understand the text.

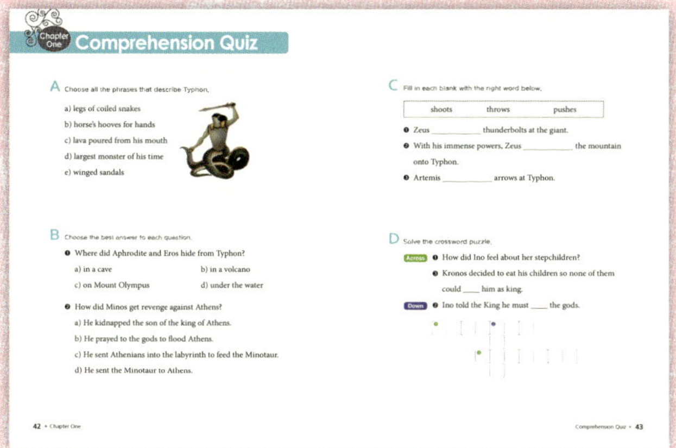

•Comprehension Quiz

After reading one chapter, solve various questions to find out if you fully understand the content.

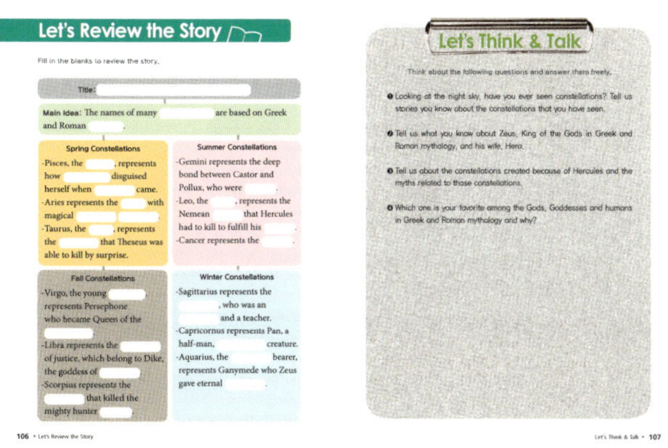

•Let's Review the Story /
•Let's Think & Talk

Fill in the blanks in the organizer to summarize the whole story. Express your own thinking and feelings about the story by answering the questions. You can build up logic and reasoning skills for your essay examinations in the future.

Appendix

Audio CD
In the CD audio book form, the texts are read vividly by American professional voice actors.

After-reading Test
Solve an additionally provided After-reading Test for each book.

The Korean translation, Answer Keys, a Word Quiz, a Word List, and Aha! Tips for each book
You can download them for free at *www.ihappyhouse.co.kr*

Before Reading

The Myths in the Stars

Level 6-3,
Lexile® 870L

•Literature〉Myths
•Story

A mysterious book about constellations that embroider the night sky

You can rarely see stars in cities, but you can often see different clusters of stars that light up the night sky if you go to the countryside. Ancient people considered the sky as a circle and divided it into 12 parts. They called the 12 parts "the zodiac." Viewed from Earth, the sun appears to pass by each of the 12 parts once a year. Within the 12 parts are 88 constellations. Ancient people wanted to hear the conversations of these constellations that had been guarding the night sky for tens of thousands of years. Especially, the Greeks' and Romans' imagination of these conversations was weaved into mythical stories about the stars. Shall we read Greek and Roman mythology about the 12 zodiac signs that embroider the spring, summer, fall and winter night sky?

Summary

People of the past planned farming or predicted the future by examining the movement of different stars or constellations. In this process, stars were named and myths were created to explain the different constellations. Myths about the 12 zodiac signs especially, that is, Pisces, Aries and Taurus that represent spring, Gemini, Leo and Cancer that represent summer, Virgo, Libra and Scorpio that represent fall, and lastly Sagittarius, Capricorn and Aquarius that represent winter are all very interesting and special. Listen carefully to the stories about Greek and Roman gods and goddesses such as the famous Zeus, Hera, Poseidon etc., who appear with heroes and monsters such as Jason, Hercules, Hydra, etc. in these myths about the constellations.

Contents

The Myths in the Stars

The Myths in the Stars

Constellations and Myths

A constellation is a group of stars that make a shape in the sky. Constellations aren't real things. They are patterns in the sky that we see from Earth.

Different patterns can be seen at different times of year and from different parts of the world. Some constellations are only visible in the Northern Hemisphere, like the Big Dipper.

KEY WORDS

- constellation
- myth
- pattern

- visible
- Northern Hemisphere
- the Big Dipper

Some can only be seen in the Southern Hemisphere, like the Southern Cross.

Farmers created constellations so they could tell the difference between seasons. Knowing the seasons told farmers when to plant and when to harvest. The myths for each constellation may have helped farmers remember them.

KEY WORDS

- the Southern Hemisphere
- the Southern Cross
- tell the difference between
- plant
- harvest

Some of the most famous constellation stories come from Greek and Roman mythology. Different stories exist in different parts of the world for the same constellations. For this reason, some constellations have many names. For example, Ursa Major is also known as the Great Bear, the Plough, and the Big Dipper. The earliest references to Greek myths as related to constellations were found in the works of Homer. Homer was an ancient Greek epic poet best known for *The Odyssey* and *The Iliad*. His references to constellations probably date to the 7th century BC. By the 5th century BC, most constellations had become attached to myths.

KEY WORDS

- Greek
- Roman
- mythology
- for this reason
- Ursa Major
- be known as
- the Great Bear
- dipper (*cf.* Big Dipper)
- plough
- a reference to
- as related to (*cf.* related)
- work
- ancient

- epic
- date
- BC (*cf.* AD)
- become attached to
- complete
- star catalogue
- belong to
- astronomer
- astrologer
- geographer
- mathematician
- group

The most complete star catalogue of ancient times belongs to a Roman poet. Ptolemy of Alexandria was a poet, astronomer, astrologer, geographer, and mathematician born around 90 AD. He grouped 1,022 stars into 48 constellations during the 2nd century AD. Ptolemy named the constellations according to Greek myths. He gave them their Roman names, however, because he was Roman.

▲ the zodiac

KEY WORDS

- astronomical
- adopt
- official
- be based on
- original
- zodiac
- movement
- be divided into
- section
- orbit
- make sure to
- Gemini
- Pisces
- Sagittarius
- Libra
- maybe
- discover
- celestial body

In 1925, the International Astronomical Union adopted 88 official constellations. These are the constellations we know today and they are based on Ptolemy's original 48 constellations.

Some of the most famous constellations are those belonging to the zodiac. The zodiac is a circle in the sky related to the sun's movements. The circle is divided into twelve sections, each named for a mythological character or object. The sun passes in front of each of the twelve sections as the Earth orbits the sun. In this book, the constellations of the zodiac are grouped according to the season in which the sun passes in front.

After reading this story, make sure to spend some time looking up at the stars when you get the chance. Maybe you'll be able to find Gemini, Pisces, Sagittarius, or Libra. Maybe you'll discover the next great celestial body!

Chapter One

Spring Constellations

♓ Pisces

Before the gods of Olympus ruled the ancient Greek world, the Titans reigned instead. The Titans were children of Ouranos, the sky father, and Gaia, the earth mother. One of the Titans, Kronos, fathered Zeus and some of the other Olympian gods. He was the king of all the gods. Kronos had planned to eat all his children as soon as they were born so that none of them could replace him as king.

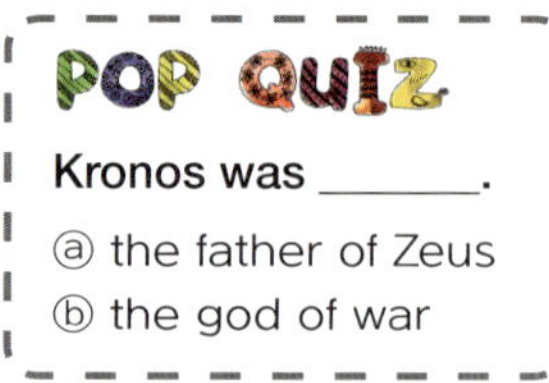

However, when Zeus was born, Kronos's wife told her husband Zeus had died and instead she hid the baby. She sent him to the island of Crete and allowed him to be raised by a nurse. Eventually, Zeus grew up and defeated Kronos and the other Titans in the Titan War.

KEY WORDS

- **reign** (= rule)
- **father**
- **the Olympian Gods**
- **as soon as**
- **replace**
- **hide** (hide-hid-hidden)
- **allow**
- **be raised by**
- **eventually**
- **grow up**
- **defeat** (= beat)

After the Titan War, Gaia was angry at the Olympian gods for defeating her children, the Titans. So she gave birth to a giant named Typhon so he could take revenge on the gods for Gaia.

Typhon was a terrible monster, the largest of his time. While some of his body looked human, his legs consisted of coiled snakes. He also had arms which had a huge reach. He had tangled hair, and lava poured from his mouth. He was so enormous and strong that he could rip mountains out of the earth to throw them at the gods.

KEY WORDS

- give birth to
- named
- take revenge on A for B (*cf.* revenge)
- terrible
- consist of
- coiled

- reach
- tangled
- lava
- pour
- enormous
- rip

Some of Typhon's children were famous monsters in Greek mythology. The Nemean Lion had invincible skin. The Hydra had many heads and poisonous blood. Cerberus was the three-headed dog who guarded the Underworld. The Sphinx guarded one of the pyramids of Egypt.

When Typhon came after the gods, they ran away and hid in the form of animals. Zeus transformed into a ram, Hermes turned himself into a kind of aquatic bird called an ibis. Apollo hid as a crow, while his sister Artemis transformed into a cat. Dionysus turned himself into a goat.

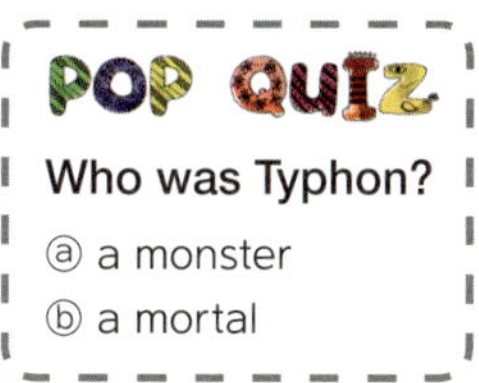

KEY WORDS

- invincible
- poisonous
- guard
- underworld
- sphinx
- come after
- run away
- transform into
- ram
- turn A into B
- aquatic
- ibis
- goat

Aphrodite, the goddess of love and beauty, had a different idea. She led her son, Eros, to the ocean. "Dive in, my son," she said. "The waves will hide our presence and keep us safe."

"How will we breathe underwater?" Eros asked.

"We are gods, the most powerful beings on Earth," she said. "We have the power to change our form into anything we want. We will disguise ourselves as fish."

So, Aphrodite and Eros dove into the water where they turned themselves into fish. They plunged deep down into the ocean and hid until the land was safe. As fish, they swam and played and met all sorts of underwater creatures. Eventually Zeus stopped running, turned around, and chose to fight the monster. The other gods stood with him and fought Typhon. Aphrodite and Eros turned themselves back into their human-like forms and joined the other gods.

KEY WORDS

- goddess
- presence
- breathe
- underwater
- disguise oneself as
- plunge
- creature
- rage on
- blind
- ray

The war between the gods and the monster raged on.
Typhon was so huge, all he had to do was step on a god
to hurt him. Artemis shot arrows at Typhon from her bow.
Apollo attempted to blind Typhon with the rays of the sun.

POP QUIZ

Aphrodite was the goddess of _______.

ⓐ fire
ⓑ love

Typhon pulled Mount Aetna out of the
ground and hurled it at Zeus. Zeus
threw thunderbolts at the giant. With
his immense powers, Zeus pushed the
mountain onto Typhon.

According to mythology, Typhon still lies
pinned under Mount Aetna today.

▲ Zeus

After the gods defeated Typhon, Aphrodite
honored all fish for allowing herself and her son to hide
among them. She put them in the sky as a constellation.
Pisces, which means "fish" in Latin, is represented by
two fish swimming in opposite directions. These two fish
represent Aphrodite and Eros.

The constellation isn't very bright and can be difficult to
locate. The sun passes through the constellation of Pisces
from February 19th to March 20th.

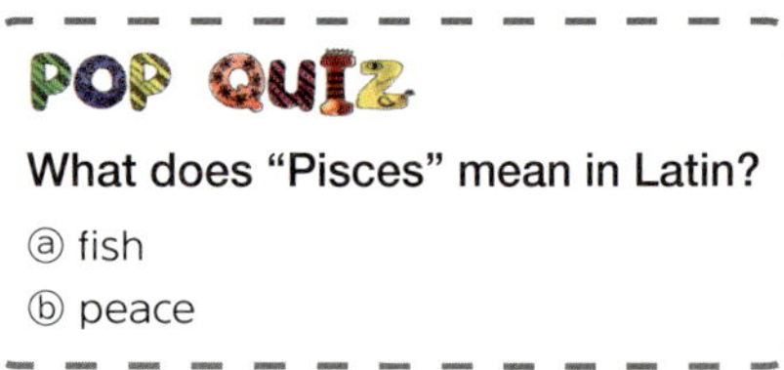

KEY WORDS

- hurl
- thunderbolt
- immense
- pin

- honor
- Latin
- be represented by
- opposite

- direction
- locate
- pass through

♈ Aries

Once upon a time in ancient Greece, there was a cloud nymph named Nephele. She had two children, named Helle and Phrixus, with a king in western Greece. The king's new wife, Ino, was jealous of her husband's children. She suspected that her husband cared more for his kids than he cared for her. Ino wanted to be a powerful queen and she didn't want to share power with anyone else, especially not with her stepchildren.

Ino devised a terrible plot in order to get the king, and the kingdom, all to herself. At harvest time, Ino convinced the women of the kingdom to plant bad wheat. The bad wheat failed to grow, which caused famine to plague the kingdom.

KEY WORDS

- nymph
- be jealous of
- suspect
- care for
- stepchild
- devise a plot
- harvest time

- convince
- wheat
- famine
- plague
- beg (beg-begged-begged)
- suffer
- suggest

"Husband, you must do something to save the people of your kingdom," Ino begged the king.

"Yes, Ino, you are right. I can't let my people continue to suffer," he said. "What do you suggest, my queen, to help our people?"

"The gods will help us if we pray to them and if you offer them a sacrifice," Ino said.

"A sacrifice will show the gods I respect and need them," the king said. "But what kind of sacrifice will they accept?"

The king sent a messenger to the famous oracle at Delphi to find out what the gods wanted in return for putting an end to the famine. The messenger returned with the awful message that the king must sacrifice his own two children.

▼ Delphi

"No, this is impossible! The gods can't ask for such an enormous and life-changing action of me," the king wailed. "How can I sacrifice my own children whom I love so dearly?"

"Husband, your people die of hunger every day. You must do as the gods demand," Ino said.

People starved to death and the kingdom continued to suffer. "If it is the will of the gods," Ino said, "then you must obey." In the end, the king felt he had no choice. As the ruler of the kingdom, he had to do whatever it took to make his people happy and prosperous. The day of the sacrifice arrived and everyone in the kingdom gathered at the palace to watch the spectacle.

KEY WORDS

- pray
- offer
- sacrifice
- accept
- messenger
- oracle
- find out
- in return for
- put an end to
- awful
- impossible

- life-changing
- wail
- dearly
- die of hunger
- starve to death
- in the end
- whatever it takes
- prosperous
- gather
- spectacle

However, Nephele would not allow her children to be killed for the sake of the kingdom or even for the gods. During the ceremony, she swooped down from the clouds and streaked toward the gathering.

"Look! Watch out," people shouted.

Everyone shielded their eyes from the sun and watched Nephele fly toward them.

"Phrixus! Helle!" she shouted as she flew to them.

She reached out her arms and snatched them out of the palace grounds. Nephele had rescued her children.

Once in a safe place, Nephele begged the god Hermes for help. Hermes was the youngest child of Zeus.

As the fastest god, he became Zeus's messenger and wore winged sandals and a winged hat. Hermes was friendly and cheerful; everyone liked him. Hermes heard Nephele's prayers and decided to help her. He sent her a magical male sheep with golden fur, called fleece.

KEY WORDS

- for the sake of
- during
- ceremony
- swoop down
- streak
- gathering

- watch out
- shield
- snatch
- rescue
- magical
- fleece

"This ram is special and will fly your children to safety,"
Hermes told her.
Nephele trusted Hermes and put her children on the back of
the golden ram.

POP QUIZ

Who saved the children of the king and Nephele?
ⓐ Ino
ⓑ Nephele

The ram flew into the sky with the
two children clinging to its back.
However, as the ram crossed
the narrow strip of water
between Europe and Asia, the
girl lost her grip on the ram and fell.
"Helle, no!" her brother yelled.
Phrixus wrapped one hand in the
ram's golden fur and reached out with
the other hand for his sister, but was unable to save her.
Helle splashed into the water and drowned. However, some
poets believe the gods turned her into a sea goddess after her
death.

Although sad and grieving, Phrixus continued his journey on
the ram's back and eventually arrived in a kingdom called
Colchis on the Black Sea. There, he sacrificed the ram to
Zeus in gratitude for his safe passage.

POP QUIZ

What does "Aries" mean?
ⓐ ram
ⓑ air

KEY WORDS

- cling to
- strip of water
- lose one's grip on
- wrap

- reach out
- splash into
- drown
- grieving

- in gratitude for
- passage
- present
- place

Phrixus presented the golden fleece of the dead ram to the king of Colchis. The king placed the fleece on a high branch of a tree in a sacred grove, guarded by a dragon who never slept. The gods put the magical golden ram in the sky as the constellation Aries. The name Aries means "ram" in Latin. The constellation Aries lies in the Northern Hemisphere. It can be found between the constellations of Taurus, Perseus, and Pisces. Aries is most visible at night in December. The sun passes through the constellation Aries from March 21st to April 20th.

♉ Taurus

The next constellation in the zodiac represents the story
of Theseus and the Minotaur. One day, a beautiful white
bull washed up on the shores of Crete, an island in the
Mediterranean. It was sent to King Minos by Poseidon, god
of the sea, as a sign. Minos had asked Poseidon for a sign to
show that Minos was meant to be the true king of Crete.
In those days, all people, even kings and queens, had
to honor the gods. One way to honor the gods was by
sacrificing animals to the gods, or anything of special
significance. If people disobeyed the gods, the gods found
ways to punish them.

KEY WORDS

- bull
- wash up
- Mediterranean
- sign
- be meant to
- in those days

- significance
- creature
- disobey
- punish
- fear
- wrath

One king was punished by having harpies, creatures that were half-women, half-bird, steal all his food. He became skinnier and skinnier because he couldn't eat anything. Everyone feared the wrath of the gods, so no one wanted to disobey the gods. If people were meant to sacrifice an animal, or anything else, they usually did.

The king and queen chose not to sacrifice the bull to the gods because they thought the bull was too beautiful to destroy. 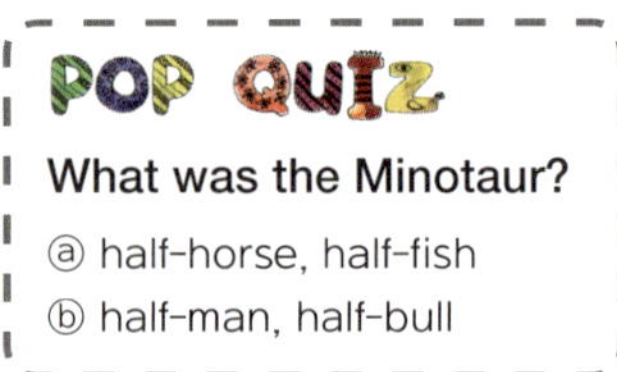 Not sacrificing the gift angered Poseidon. To punish them, Poseidon made the queen fall in love with the bull and later, she gave birth to a creature that was half man and half bull. This was the Minotaur.

The Minotaur had the lower body of a bull, the chest and arms of a man, and the head of a bull. This creature was very strong and very scary and even had horns.

King Minos couldn't kill the Minotaur, since he was the son of Minos's wife. So he kept the creature in a famous labyrinth on the island of Crete. This maze was so complicated and so difficult that no one could ever find their way out.

Minos found a way to feed the Minotaur and get revenge on the city of Athens at the same time. King Minos's first child, a human son, was killed in Athens, so Minos held a grudge against the city.

POP QUIZ

What was the Minotaur?
ⓐ half-horse, half-fish
ⓑ half-man, half-bull

KEY WORDS

- destroy
- anger
- fall in love with
- lower body
- chest
- horn

- labyrinth (= maze)
- complicated
- feed
- get revenge on
- hold a grudge against

Minos's son went to Athens to compete in the ancient Olympics. The son did well in many events, but his success made other athletes envious. A jealous athlete murdered the prince of Crete. Minos attacked Athens and won control of the city. In exchange for peace, Minos demanded a sacrifice. Seven young men and seven young women from Athens would travel across the sea to Crete every nine years. These people were then sealed into the labyrinth and eaten by the Minotaur.

One year, Theseus volunteered to be one of the seven Athenian men. Theseus was a prince of Athens, son of the king, and one of the great heroes of Greek mythology. Theseus vowed to kill the Minotaur and stop Minos's revenge on Athens.

Once in Crete, Theseus met Minos's daughter, Ariadne. The princess fell in love with Theseus and asked him to meet with her secretly.

"Take this string, Theseus," Ariadne said. "It will help you navigate your way safely through the labyrinth."

KEY WORDS

- compete in
- envious (= jealous)
- jealous
- athlete
- murder
- win control of
- in exchange for
- demand
- seal
- volunteer
- vow
- secretly
- string
- navigate one's way through

Theseus held the string and stared down at it, confused. "How will some simple string help me?"

"I used it as a child when I played in the labyrinth, which I did almost every day," Ariadne said. "It was given to me by the architect of the labyrinth."

"What do I do with it?" Theseus asked.

"Tie one end of the string to the gate at the entrance of the labyrinth and tie the other end to your wrist or around your waist," Ariadne explained. "Then, you can follow the string back to the front gate when you're ready."

Theseus did as Ariadne suggested. Holding the string, he found the Minotaur.  The sacrifices from Athens weren't allowed to bring weapons into the labyrinth, but Theseus was able to take the beast by surprise. He snuck up on the Minotaur, jumped on the creature's back, and strangled him from behind.

- stare
- confused
- architect
- tie
- entrance
- the other end
- wrist

- waist
- follow
- weapon
- take ~ by surprise
- sneak up on (sneak-snuck-snuck / sneak-sneaked-sneaked)
- strangle

The Minotaur thrashed around, but he couldn't throw
Theseus off his back. Theseus killed the Minotaur, as he
promised his father, the King of Athens, he would.
Thanks to Ariadne's string, Theseus found his way out of the
maze.  The other sacrifices followed Theseus, therefore
they were all saved. Theseus returned to Athens as a hero.
To commemorate this adventure, the gods put the Minotaur
in the sky in the form of the constellation represented by a
bull. The name Taurus means "bull" in Latin.

KEY WORDS

- thrash around
- throw off
- thanks to

- commemorate
- galaxy

Taurus is visible in the Northern Hemisphere in the winter, from November to March. It is most visible in January. Taurus is one of the oldest and most visible constellations in the galaxy. The sun passes through the constellation Taurus from April 20th to May 21st.

POP QUIZ

What does "Taurus" mean in Latin?

ⓐ bull

ⓑ horse

A Choose all the phrases that describe Typhon.

a) legs of coiled snakes

b) horse's hooves for hands

c) lava poured from his mouth

d) largest monster of his time

e) winged sandals

B Choose the best answer to each question.

❶ Where did Aphrodite and Eros hide from Typhon?

a) in a cave

b) in a volcano

c) on Mount Olympus

d) under the water

❷ How did Minos get revenge against Athens?

a) He kidnapped the son of the king of Athens.

b) He prayed to the gods to flood Athens.

c) He sent Athenians into the labyrinth to feed the Minotaur.

d) He sent the Minotaur to Athens.

C Fill in each blank with the right word below.

| shoots | throws | pushes |

❶ Zeus ______________ thunderbolts at the giant.

❷ With his immense powers, Zeus ______________ the mountain onto Typhon.

❸ Artemis ______________ arrows at Typhon.

D Solve the crossword puzzle.

Across **❶** How did Ino feel about her stepchildren?

❸ Kronos decided to eat his children so none of them could _____ him as king.

Down **❷** Ino told the King he must _____ the gods.

Chapter Two

Summer Constellations

Ⅱ Gemini

The Gemini constellation represents twins, and the word means "twins" in Latin.

The twins were Castor and Pollux. Although brothers, they were not truly twins since they had different fathers. Castor was the mortal son of a king and queen, while Pollux was the divine son of the queen and Zeus. They did everything together and were inseparable as they grew up.

KEY WORDS

- twins
- although
- truly
- mortal
- divine
- inseparable
- brother-in-law
- upper body

Castor and Pollux were two members of Jason's Argonauts.
Jason was another of Greek mythology's great heroes.
Jason's father was a king of Greece, killed by his brother.
Worried that her brother-in-law would kill her son, Jason's
mother sent him to be trained by Chiron the centaur.
A centaur is a creature with the body and legs of a horse, but
the upper body and head of a man.

When Jason turned twenty, he confronted his uncle and asked for his father's throne back.

"You are still only a boy," Uncle Pelias said. "You must prove your worth, prove you are ready to be king."

Jason stood up straight. "The throne should already be mine, Uncle. I have studied hard and learned from the best. I promise you that I am worthy."

"Then it will be easy enough for you to accomplish the task I have in mind for you, Jason," Uncle Pelias said.

KEY WORDS

- turn twenty
- confront
- throne
- prove
- worth
- stand up straight (stand-stood-stood)
- worthy
- accomplish
- task
- have in mind
- retrieve
- fearsome
- protect
- layer
- protection

"What task?" Jason asked.

Uncle Pelias smiled. "Retrieve the Golden Fleece from the king of Colchis."

A fearsome dragon guarded the Golden Fleece. The king believed that if he lost the fleece, he would lose his kingdom, so he protected the fleece. Layers of protection made this a difficult task. King Pelias didn't think Jason would succeed, so he wouldn't have to give Jason the kingdom.

Jason knew the task would be very difficult, but he had to try. He wanted his father's kingdom back.

"Okay, Uncle, I will sail to Colchis and retrieve the Golden Fleece," Jason agreed.

Jason commissioned a man named Argo to build a ship. The ship was also called the Argo, after its creator. Jason brought together a crew of heroes, called the Argonauts for the name of the ship.

Together, Jason and the Argonauts sailed off to find the Golden Fleece and had many adventures along the way. Castor and Pollux were part of the quest for the Golden Fleece as Argonauts. Pollux, as the son of a god, was immortal and known for his strength. His mortal brother Castor was famous for his skill with horses.

The brothers are traditionally depicted as armed with spears and riding a matching pair of white horses.

KEY WORDS

- agree
- commission
- creator
- bring together
- crew
- Argonaut
- sail off
- quest
- strength
- be famous for

- traditionally
- depict
- armed with
- spear
- a matching pair of
- heartbroken
- reject
- invitation

When Castor died, Pollux was heartbroken. Although the son of a god, Pollux rejected Zeus's invitation to come to Olympus to live with the Greek gods.

Zeus, impressed by Pollux's grief for his brother, made the brothers an incredible offer. Since he was dead, Castor would normally have to stay in the Underworld, and since Pollux was still alive, he wasn't normally allowed in the Underworld. But Zeus allowed both brothers to stay together, splitting their time between the Underworld and Olympus. Zeus also put them in the skies. Castor and Pollux are unlike other heroes placed in the sky as a constellation because there are actual stars in the Gemini constellation named "Castor" and "Pollux." Castor is a bright white binary star, while Pollux is orange.

In life, Poseidon made the twins saviors of shipwrecked sailors and granted them the power to send favorable winds whenever they wished. Sailors consider the sight of their constellation as a good omen.

The constellation is between Taurus and Cancer, near Orion. It is best viewed at night in February. The sun shines through the constellation Gemini from June 16th to July 15th.

KEY WORDS

- impressed by
- incredible
- offer
- normally
- split
- unlike
- actual
- binary star
- in life
- savior
- shipwrecked
- sailor
- grant
- favorable
- consider
- good omen
- view

POP QUIZ

The twins were saviors of ____.

ⓐ lame horses
ⓑ shipwrecked sailors

The next zodiac constellation, Leo, is linked to the first labor of Hercules.

Hercules was one of Greek and Roman mythology's greatest heroes and the most talked about hero in ancient times. More stories were told of Hercules than of Jason, or Theseus, or Castor and Pollux. Hercules was the son of Zeus and a mortal woman. Hera, queen of the gods and Zeus's wife, bothered Hercules throughout his life out of jealousy. 🌐 His Greek name, Heracles, means "glory of Hera." Zeus hoped the name would help Hera to accept his child, but it did not work.

▲ Hera

When Hercules was a baby, Hera sent two snakes into the crib he shared with his brother. Hercules killed the snakes, saved his brother's life and his own, thus beginning his career as a monster-killer.

KEY WORDS

- be linked to
- labor
- crib

- share with
- career

Later, Hercules married a princess of Thebes. Unfortunately, Hera drove Hercules mad and he killed his wife and children. As punishment, he was sent to perform the twelve labors that made him famous.

Each labor was a task that would have proven impossible for anyone else. The first labor of Hercules was to get rid of the Nemean Lion. The Nemean Lion had skin that was resistant to all man-made weapons. Its skin couldn't be pierced by iron, stone, or bronze.

Twice the size of a normal lion, it terrorized the countryside of Nemea. The people of Nemea couldn't kill the lion, and couldn't keep it from eating them and their cattle.  The lion was the son of the monster Typhon who fought the gods on the side of the Titans.

POP QUIZ

What was the first labor?

ⓐ to kill the Nemean Lion
ⓑ to retrieve the Golden Fleece

KEY WORDS

- unfortunately
- drive ~ mad
- punishment
- perform

- get rid of
- resistant
- man-made
- pierce

- terrorize
- countryside
- cattle

Since his arrows didn't work against the lion's impenetrable hide, Hercules trapped the lion in a cave. Once cornered, Hercules hit the lion with his club to stun it, then strangled it with his bare hands.

KEY WORDS

- impenetrable
- hide (= skin, leather)
- trap
- corner
- stun
- bare hand

To prove the lion's death, Hercules had to skin the lion and bring the lion's pelt to the king who had sent him on the labor. Since no weapon could pierce the skin, Hercules had to find a more creative way to skin the lion. Hercules thought and thought about what to do.

"My weapons won't pierce the skin, but its claws are sharp," he said to himself. "I wonder if the lion's claws will cut through its hide."

So he removed one of the dead lion's claws and used it to skin the lion. Hercules wore the lion's pelt like armor because it couldn't be penetrated by any weapon. It was the safest armor of the time.

In artwork, Hercules is usually pictured with the lion's skin worn like a cloak.

KEY WORDS

- skin
- pelt
- claw
- wonder if
- cut through
- remove

- armor
- penetrate
- artwork
- picture
- cloak
- location

Leo is Latin for "lion." Hera chose to honor the lion's sacrifice by putting it among the stars.

The constellation is one of the easiest to find in the sky. The Big Dipper points south toward the location of Leo's brightest star, a bright blue-white star named Regulus in Leo's chest. The constellation is visible in the Northern Hemisphere from late March through May. The best time to view Leo is at night in April. The constellation Leo lies between Virgo and Cancer. The sun passes in front of Leo from August 10th to September 16th.

♋ Cancer

The constellation of Cancer is related to
the second labor of Hercules, in which
Hercules was sent to kill the Hydra,
a water serpent with nine heads.
The Hydra had terrorized people in the
swamps of Lerna for many years. It
devoured entire herds of cattle and local
villagers. There is a constellation called
Hydra, in honor of this serpent and
his fight with Hercules. There is also a
constellation in honor of Hercules, the
hero. The Hydra was a difficult monster
to fight. Whenever Hercules cut off one of
its heads, two would grow in its place.
Hercules had the idea to burn the stumps
after cutting off a head, which would
keep a new head from growing. But
Hercules couldn't do it all by himself.
Luckily, Hercules's nephew came on this quest with him.

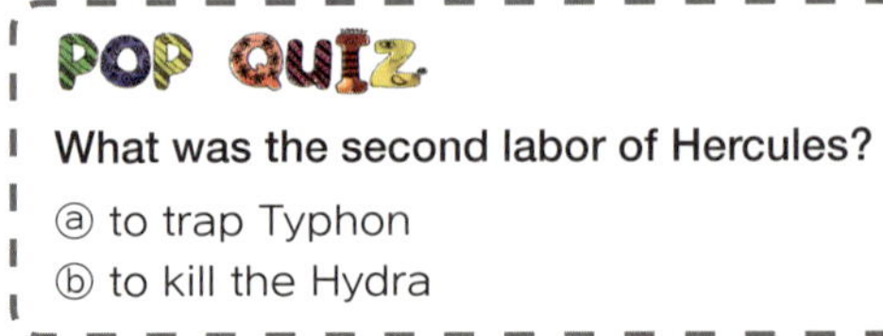

POP QUIZ

What was the second labor of Hercules?

ⓐ to trap Typhon
ⓑ to kill the Hydra

KEY WORDS

- be related to
- serpent
- swamp
- devour

- entire
- herd
- local
- villager

- cut off
- in one's place
- stump
- luckily

"Iolaus!" Hercules called to his nephew. "Light the torch and bring it here."

Iolaus did as he was told and Hercules explained his idea. While Hercules cut off one of the Hydra's heads, other heads would nip at his legs. Hercules bashed the heads away from his legs with his club, preventing the Hydra from biting him and sending poison through his blood stream.

Then, Hercules cut off one of the Hydra's heads. While Hercules would turn his attention to the next head, Iolaus held the fire to the stump. One by one, they cut off all of the Hydra's heads and prevented any new ones from growing.

▲ Hercules

When the goddess Hera realized Hercules could defeat the Hydra, she got very angry. She had to do something to stop Hercules, so she sent a giant crab to help the Hydra. The crab bit Hercules on the foot and attempted to distract him.

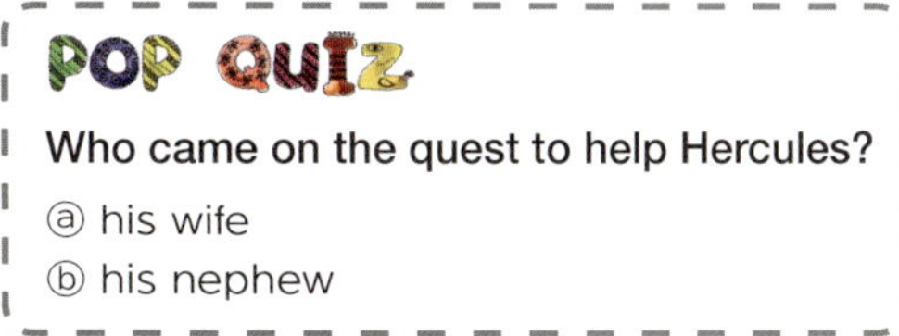

KEY WORDS

- torch
- nip
- bash
- poison

- blood stream
- one by one
- turn one's attention to
- distract

However, even a giant crab was no match for the greatest Greek hero. Hercules killed the crab by crushing it with his heel. Hera honored the crab's service anyway by placing it among the stars.

Cancer is Latin for "crab."

The constellation Cancer lies between Leo and Gemini, but it is almost impossible to see even with binoculars because it is too faint. In fact, Cancer is the least brightest of all the zodiac constellations. 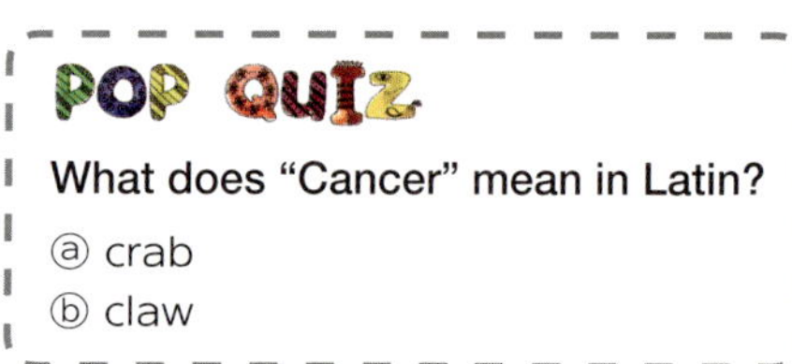

According to mythology, Hera placed the crab between two bright constellations on purpose. The goddess honored the crab's service, but since he failed in his mission, she gave him a poor location.

KEY WORDS

- be no match for
- crush
- binoculars
- faint

- in fact
- on purpose
- mission
- visibility

Cancer can be seen in the Northern Hemisphere in the early spring, and in the Southern Hemisphere in the fall. The best visibility in the Northern Hemisphere is at night in March. The sun passes in front of the constellation from July 20th to August 10th.

A Choose all the words that describe Hercules.

hero   glory of Hera

monster-killer   most handsome

son of Zeus   weak

B Mark T for true or F for false.

❶ Pollux was known for his beauty.   T F

❷ Castor and Pollux are both stars and a constellation.   T F

❸ Leo is one of the easiest zodiac constellations to find.   T F

❹ Cancer is the brightest of all the zodiac constellations.   T F

 Choose the best answer to each question.

❶ Who were the Argonauts?

a) heroes who went on a quest with Jason

b) people who helped build Rome

c) workmen who built Jason's ship

d) men guarding the king of Colchis

❷ Why did the king protect the Golden Fleece?

a) The Golden Fleece kept him warm.

b) He thought it protected his kingdom.

c) He loved using the Fleece as a rug.

d) Zeus asked the king to protect it.

❸ What did Hera do to the baby Hercules?

a) She admired his beauty.

b) She sent a scorpion to sting him.

c) She sent snakes into his crib.

d) She tickled him with a feather.

Fall Constellations

♍ Virgo

The constellation of Virgo relates to the story of Demeter and her daughter, Persephone. Their myth explains the changing of the seasons. Demeter was the goddess of the harvest, one of Zeus's sisters, and the mother of Persephone and Dionysus.

One day, Persephone was playing in a field filled with flowers. A golden chariot appeared out of the sky and landed near her. Hades, god of the Underworld, stepped out of the chariot.

"Persephone, my dear," Hades said, reaching out his hand. "Join me in the Underworld and be my queen." Hades had fallen in love with Persephone and wanted to spend eternity with her.

Persephone was confused because she had not spent much time with Hades. Also, she loved fields full of flowers, the feel of rain on her skin, and the sunlight. She didn't want to spend her life underground.

"You will rule the dead by my side," Hades continued.

Persephone was already a goddess, but now she could be a queen. Hades convinced her to leave life above ground in her past, and to become his wife. 🌐 Everything had happened so quickly. Persephone left with Hades the same day, and her mother didn't know the truth.

▲ Cerberus, the three-headed dog, guards the entrance of the Greek Underworld.

Demeter wandered the mortal world looking for her daughter, asking everyone she met if they had seen Persephone. Demeter neglected her duties as goddess of the harvest, which caused plants to die and eventually, famine set in.

After too long a period of human suffering, Zeus stepped in and sent a messenger to the Underworld. Someone had to convince Hades to let Persephone go, so Demeter would do her important job. Demeter would only allow crops to grow again if she could see her daughter.

KEY WORDS

- above ground
- wander
- look for
- neglect

- duty
- set in
- period
- suffering

- step in
- crop

The messenger arrived in the Underworld and delivered
Zeus's message. Hades wasn't happy, but he didn't want to
anger Zeus or make his bride unhappy.

KEY WORDS

- arrive in
- deliver

Hades agreed to let his bride return to the surface if she chose.

"My dearest Persephone, before you leave, eat this pomegranate," Hades said to her. "Have a little snack." Of course, his gift wasn't innocent because he didn't really want her to leave. The number of pomegranate seeds she ate would determine how long she could remain above ground.

Persephone thanked her husband for what she believed was a thoughtful gift. 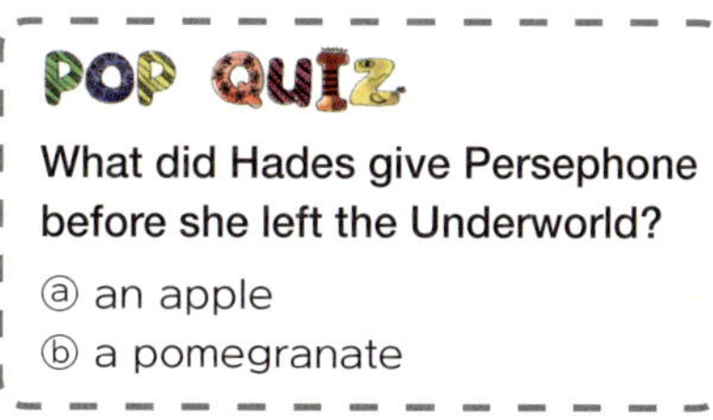

Before leaving the Underworld, she ate six pomegranate seeds. This meant she would spend six months – spring and summer – with her mother above ground. She would spend the rest of the year – fall and winter – as goddess of the dead.

This is how we got the changing of the seasons and the cycles of nature. Demeter was happy when her daughter visited and made flowers and crops grow. The sun shone brightly, the air was warm, and the world enjoyed spring and summer.

POP QUIZ

What did Hades give Persephone before she left the Underworld?

ⓐ an apple
ⓑ a pomegranate

KEY WORDS

- surface
- pomegranate
- innocent
- seed
- determine

- remain
- thoughtful
- the rest of
- the cycle of nature
- brightly

When Persephone returned to the Underworld, however, Demeter's sadness made the plants die off, as they do in the fall and winter. The weather became cold, crops didn't grow, and sometimes snow even fell and ice covered the ground. Virgo means "young maiden" in Latin. The gods put Persephone among the stars to honor her duties as Queen of the Underworld.

Virgo is the second largest constellation, and the largest zodiac constellation. It is highest in the Northern Hemisphere during May and June. Virgo is visible in the night sky from late April through August and can also be seen in the Southern Hemisphere.

The Virgo constellation is easy to locate by following the arc of the handle of the Big Dipper to Spica. Spica, a sparkling blue-white star, is the brightest star in Virgo.

The sun passes in front of the constellation Virgo from September 16th to October 30th.

KEY WORDS

- die off
- cover
- maiden
- arc
- handle
- sparkling

♎ Libra

The next constellation is Libra which is the only zodiac sign that doesn't represent an animal or person. Instead, the constellation represents the scales of justice, which in turn symbolize equity and balance. Today, the scales of justice are used to show the fairness of laws.

Scales work by balancing an equal amount of weight on each side. Day and night are equal when the sun shines through the constellation of Libra. The scales may have belonged to Dike, goddess of justice. She was the daughter of Zeus and a Titan named Themis.

KEY WORDS

- zodiac sign
- scales
- justice
- in turn
- symbolize
- equity
- balance

- fairness
- equal
- an amount of
- weight
- tend
- peacefully

A very long time ago, Dike lived on earth among mortals when there was no war, and people tended their fields and lived peacefully.

POP QUIZ

What does Libra represent?

ⓐ the book of life

ⓑ the scales of justice

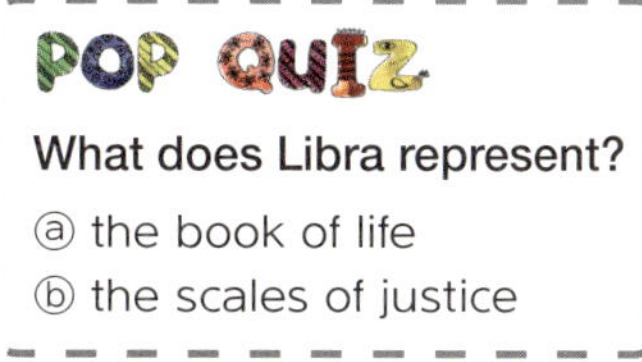

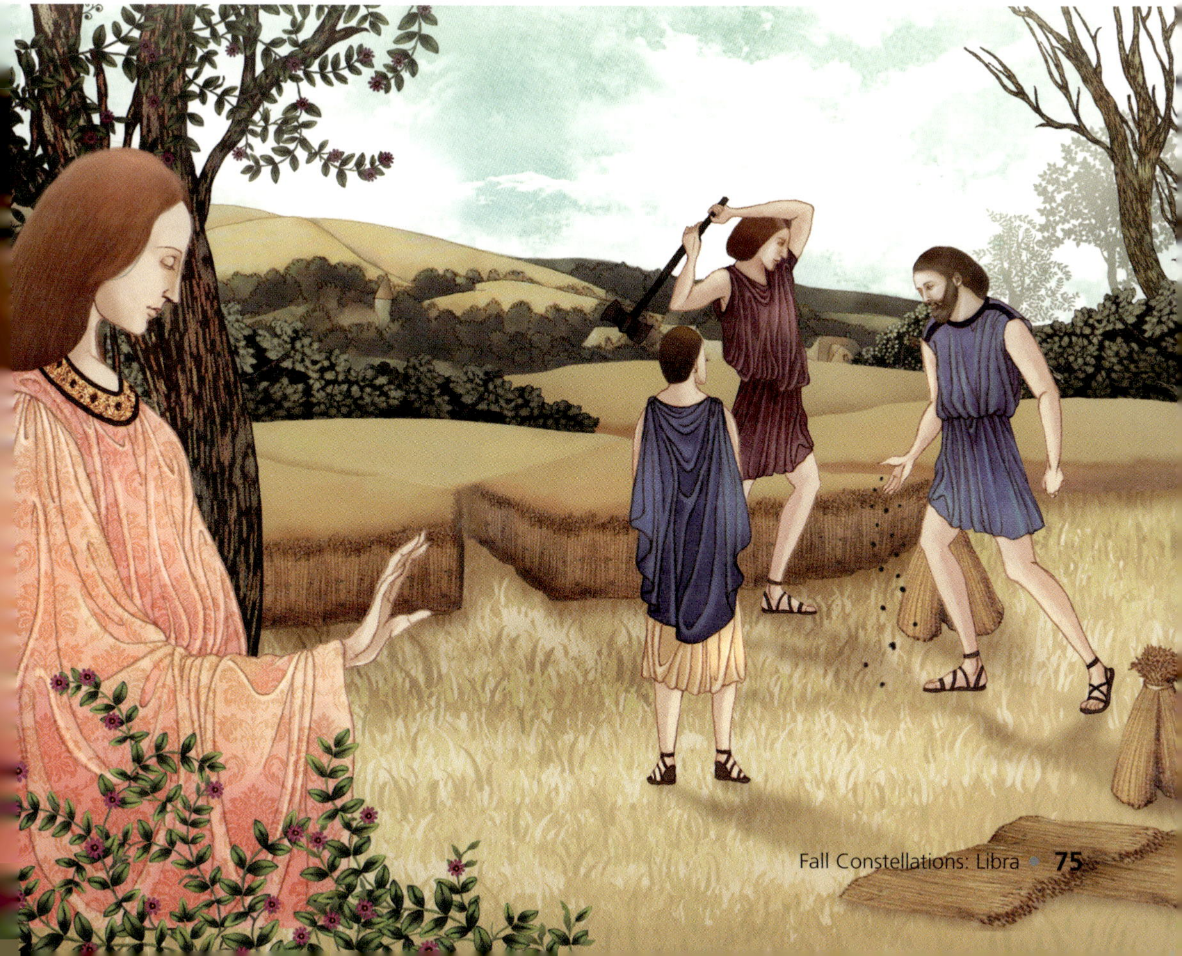

Eventually people became greedy and waged war and this made Dike unhappy. She chose to leave the greed and chaos of Earth and remain in the heavens instead.

Libra is represented in the sky next to the hand of Virgo. The Romans liked Libra in particular because they believed the Moon was in Libra when Rome was founded. This means that the Moon was visible in the constellation of Libra at the time of Rome's creation.

Libra means "weighing scales" in Latin.

This constellation lies in the Southern Hemisphere between Virgo and Scorpius, and near Lupus and Hydra. Libra is most visible at night in June, but it is a faint constellation. The sun passes through Libra between October 16th and November 15th.

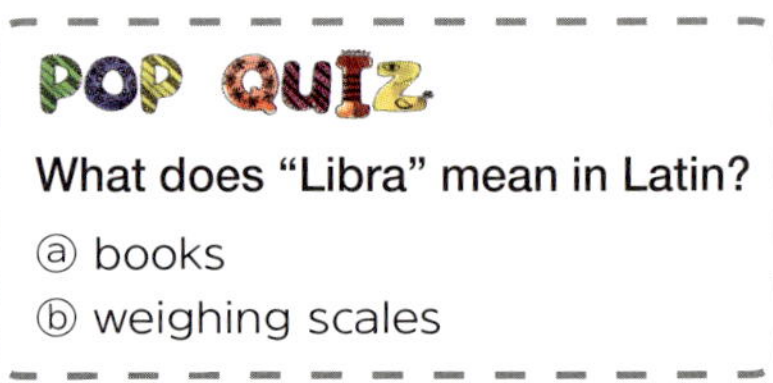

KEY WORDS

- greedy
- wage war
- greed
- chaos
- the heavens

- in particular
- found (found-founded-founded)
- weighing scales
- Lupus
- Scorpius

♏ Scorpius

The constellation of Scorpius is linked to
the hero Orion, who was the son of the
sea-god Poseidon and an Amazon queen.
The Amazons were a race of warrior
women who hated men and may have
been descendants of Ares, the god of war.
Amazons were strong and fierce, and they

▲ Poseidon

fought on horseback with bows and arrows. They also used
swords, axes, and crescent-shaped shields.
Amazons were known throughout ancient Greece as
fighters and hunters. Not surprisingly, these warrior women
worshiped the god of war and the goddess of the hunt.
From his mother, Orion inherited a talent for hunting. Orion
was said to be the tallest and most handsome man of the
known world. He was often seen hunting in the woods and
hills of ancient Greece with his pack of dogs.

KEY WORDS

- Poseidon
- race
- warrior
- descendant
- Ares
- fierce
- on horseback

- bow
- arrow
- sword
- axe
- crescent-shaped
- shield
- throughout

- not surprisingly
- worship
- inherit
- talent
- the known world
- pack of

Unfortunately, along with his enormous strength came
a huge ego. Orion became the companion of the hunting
goddess, Artemis.

One day while hunting with Artemis, Orion stopped in his
tracks. "I know I can capture any animal on earth."

Artemis tried to shush him. "You shouldn't say such things,
Orion. You will anger Mother Earth."

"But no creature exists on Earth that I can't beat," he boasted. He wasn't worried about Mother Earth retaliating against him because he knew he was right.

"I can capture or kill any living beast because I am that good a hunter."

In response, Gaea, the earth goddess, also known as Mother Earth, sent a scorpion after him. The mighty Orion was killed by the sting of the scorpion, a creature much smaller than the great hunter.

KEY WORDS

- along with
- ego
- companion
- Artemis
- in one's tracks
- capture
- shush
- beat
- boast
- retaliate against
- that
- in response
- Gaea
- scorpion
- mighty
- sting

Scorpius is Latin for "scorpion." Both Orion and the scorpion were honored with constellations. Artemis placed Orion and his hunting dogs in the sky out of her love for him and Gaea honored the scorpion by placing him in the sky, too. Scorpius is one of the brightest constellations in the sky and can be seen from both hemispheres. In the Northern Hemisphere, it lies near the southern horizon; in the Southern Hemisphere, Scorpius is high in the sky near the middle of the Milky Way.

Orion and the scorpion who killed him are on opposite sides of the sky. Some say this is so the scorpion can never hurt Orion again. The two constellations cannot be seen at the same time.

Scorpius can best be seen at night in July in both hemispheres. It is near Libra and Sagittarius. The sun passes in front of the constellation Scorpius only for one week, from November 23rd through 30th.

KEY WORDS

- horizon
- Milky Way

Chapter Three: Comprehension Quiz

A Choose all the words that describe Orion.

tallest

fiercest

most handsome

bravest

strongest

most selfish

B Fill in each blank with the correct past form of the verb below.

choose	become	make	wage

❶ Eventually people ______________ greedy.

❷ They ______________ war.

❸ This ______________ Dike unhappy.

❹ She ______________ to leave the greed and chaos of Earth.

 Mark T for true or F for false.

❶ Hades wouldn't let Persephone leave the Underworld. T F

❷ Persephone is only the goddess of the Underworld in fall and winter. T F

❸ Dike was a daughter of Zeus. T F

❹ Orion and the scorpion can be seen in the sky at the same time. T F

D Choose the best answer to each question.

❶ What did Hades want to do with Persephone?

a) to help her take over Olympus

b) to hurt her

c) to marry her

d) to pick flowers with her

❷ Who was Orion often seen hunting with in the hills?

a) Apollo

b) Gaea

c) Hercules

d) his pack of dogs

Winter Constellations

↗ Sagittarius

Once upon a time, there was a famous centaur named Chiron who inspired several constellations. Chiron was the son of the Titan Kronos and a princess, and was educated by the gods Apollo and Artemis. He was the teacher of great heroes such as Achilles, Jason, and Hercules. He was an excellent archer, musician, and doctor. Chiron was well-known throughout ancient Greece and was greatly respected. One day, while returning from one of his twelve labors, Hercules was attacked by a group of unruly centaurs. Unlike Chiron, most centaurs were wild creatures who drank too much and robbed travelers. Chiron bravely galloped into the fray to save his friend. "Stop fighting, my brother centaurs! Please, leave my friend, Hercules, alone. He's not a danger to any of you."

KEY WORDS

- centaur
- inspire
- educate
- excellent
- archer
- greatly
- respect

- unruly
- rob
- traveler
- bravely
- gallop
- fray

The centaurs didn't stop shooting arrows at Hercules. Their war whoops were too loud to hear Chiron's protests. Hercules had no choice but to fight back with his arrows which had been dipped in the Hydra's poison. He lifted his bow and nocked an arrow, and let the arrow fly. It flew straight and true into the crowd of centaurs.

When the crowd parted, Hercules saw with horror that his arrow had wounded his old teacher, Chiron. Hercules wasn't punished, since he lived in a time when men often had to defend themselves from thieves and bandits, and he had not meant to harm Chiron.

As an immortal, Chiron couldn't die, so instead was left in extreme agony from the Hydra's poison. Rather than live forever in so much pain, Chiron wanted to give up his immortality. Becoming mortal would allow him to die and end his suffering.

KEY WORDS

- war whoop
- protest
- fight back
- dip
- nock an arrow
- straight
- true
- part

- with horror
- wound
- defend
- bandit
- harm
- agony
- give up
- immortality

Chiron offered to give up his
immortality for Prometheus's freedom.
Prometheus was a Titan who had
stolen fire from the gods and gave
it to humans. The gods punished
Prometheus by chaining him to
a rock and allowing an eagle
to eat his liver every day.
Each night his liver would
grow back so the torture could last forever.
Hercules couldn't bear to see his old friend and mentor,
Chiron, in such pain.
Hercules begged Zeus, "Father, please let Chiron take
Prometheus's place and so end the suffering of both men."
Zeus considered the matter. "I will release Prometheus from
his chains," Zeus said. "The Titan has been punished long
enough. I will take Chiron's immortality instead."

KEY WORDS

- freedom
- chain
- liver
- torture
- last
- forever
- cannot bear to
- mentor
- take one's place
- matter
- release
- in recognition of
- dense
- run through
- border
- Capricornus
- Aqulia

Thus, Chiron gave up his immortality and was able to die. In recognition of his sacrifice and his friendship to Hercules, Zeus put Chiron in the sky. Sagittarius means "archer" in Latin.

Sagittarius lies low in the southern sky and is best viewed on August nights. The densest part of the Milky Way runs through this constellation. Sagittarius is the largest constellation in the Southern Hemisphere.

The Sagittarius constellation borders Capricornus, Scorpius, and Aquila. The sun passes in front of the constellation Sagittarius from December 18th to January 20th.

♑ Capricornus

The next constellation is Capricornus, which
represents a creature that is a mix of goat and
fish. Capricornus has to do with Pan, the god
of nature. Pan had mostly the form of a human,
but also the legs and horns of a goat, and
was known for his thick beard. Pan wandered
the mountains playing his pan-pipes, a kind
of wooden musical instrument named for
him, and chasing nymphs. Unfortunately, the
nymphs thought he was ugly, so they always
ran away.

Pan played an important role during the War of
the Titans. When Typhon came after the
gods, Pan blew his pipes to warn the gods.
He blew through the pipes with all the air in
his lungs.

"My brothers, the monster Typhon is coming!" he yelled.
The gods scattered in all directions.

"Run and hide and disguise yourselves as animals," Pan said.

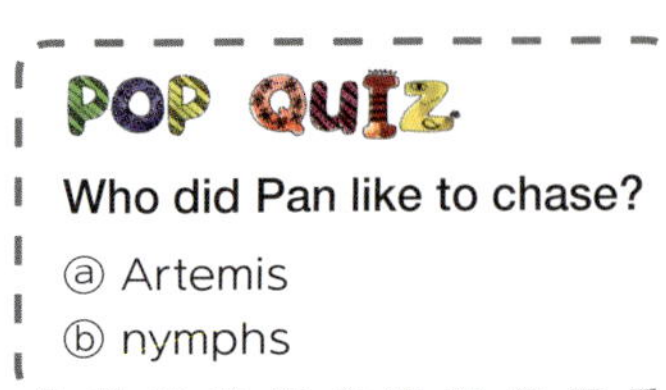

KEY WORDS

- have to do with
- mostly
- form
- beard
- pan-pipes
- wooden
- musical instrument

- chase
- play a role
- **blow** (blow-blew-blown)
- lung
- scatter
- in all directions

When Typhon came, Pan dove into a river, but the monster
scared Pan so much that he didn't disguise himself well.
The part of him that was below the water transformed into
a fish, while his upper body took the form of a goat. He was
so scared that he wasn't able to fully transform himself into
a fish.

KEY WORDS

- **dive into** (dive-dove[dived]-dived)
- **scare**
- **take the form of**
- **transform A into B**
- **thunder**
- **past**
- **ignore**

The word "panic" comes from this mistake when Pan tried to hide from Typhon.

"Oh no," Pan said to himself. "My head didn't become a fish's head so I won't be able to breathe underwater. How will I stay safe from Typhon?"

When Typhon thundered past looking for Zeus, he ignored the goat head in the water. Pan stayed in the water, safe from Typhon, until Zeus confronted the monster.

During the fight, Zeus was disabled and dismembered by Typhon, and Typhon scattered Zeus's body parts around the world. Pan set off to recover all of Zeus's stolen body parts. Since Zeus was immortal, he just needed his body parts brought back together in order to heal.

It took a long time, but Pan found them all. Zeus became whole again and healed, and was then able to confront Typhon and defeat the monster. For all Pan's service during the war, Zeus awarded him by placing him among the stars.

KEY WORDS

- disable
- dismember
- set off
- recover
- stolen
- bring back together
- heal
- award
- Aquarius
- Cetus

Capricornus is Latin for "goat horn." The Capricornus constellation lies in the Southern Hemisphere, low in the southern sky. Capricornus is the second faintest constellation in the sky, after Cancer. Best viewing of Capricornus is at night in September. Capricornus may be found between Aquarius and Sagittarius, and near Cetus and Pisces. The sun passes in front of Capricornus from January 19th to February 16th.

∿∿ Aquarius

Lastly is the constellation of Aquarius, which means "water bearer" in Latin. Ganymede was the beautiful son of the first king of Troy, a city in ancient Greece which was famous for the Trojan War and the Trojan horse.

Zeus caught a glimpse of Ganymede herding his sheep on Mount Ida and couldn't get the boy out of his thoughts.

"My goodness, that is a beautiful boy," Zeus thought, watching Ganymede with the sheep. "I need a new cup-bearer and maybe this boy would be good at that job."

Zeus sent an eagle, one of his usual messengers, to fetch Ganymede and carry him to Olympus. When he arrived, Zeus greeted him with a smile. "Hello, Ganymede, shepherd and prince of Troy. Welcome to Mount Olympus, the home to all the gods of Greece. Would you like to join us?"

KEY WORDS

- lastly
- bearer
- the Trojan War
- the Trojan horse
- catch a glimpse of
- herd
- my goodness
- cup-bearer
- be good at
- usual
- fetch
- greet

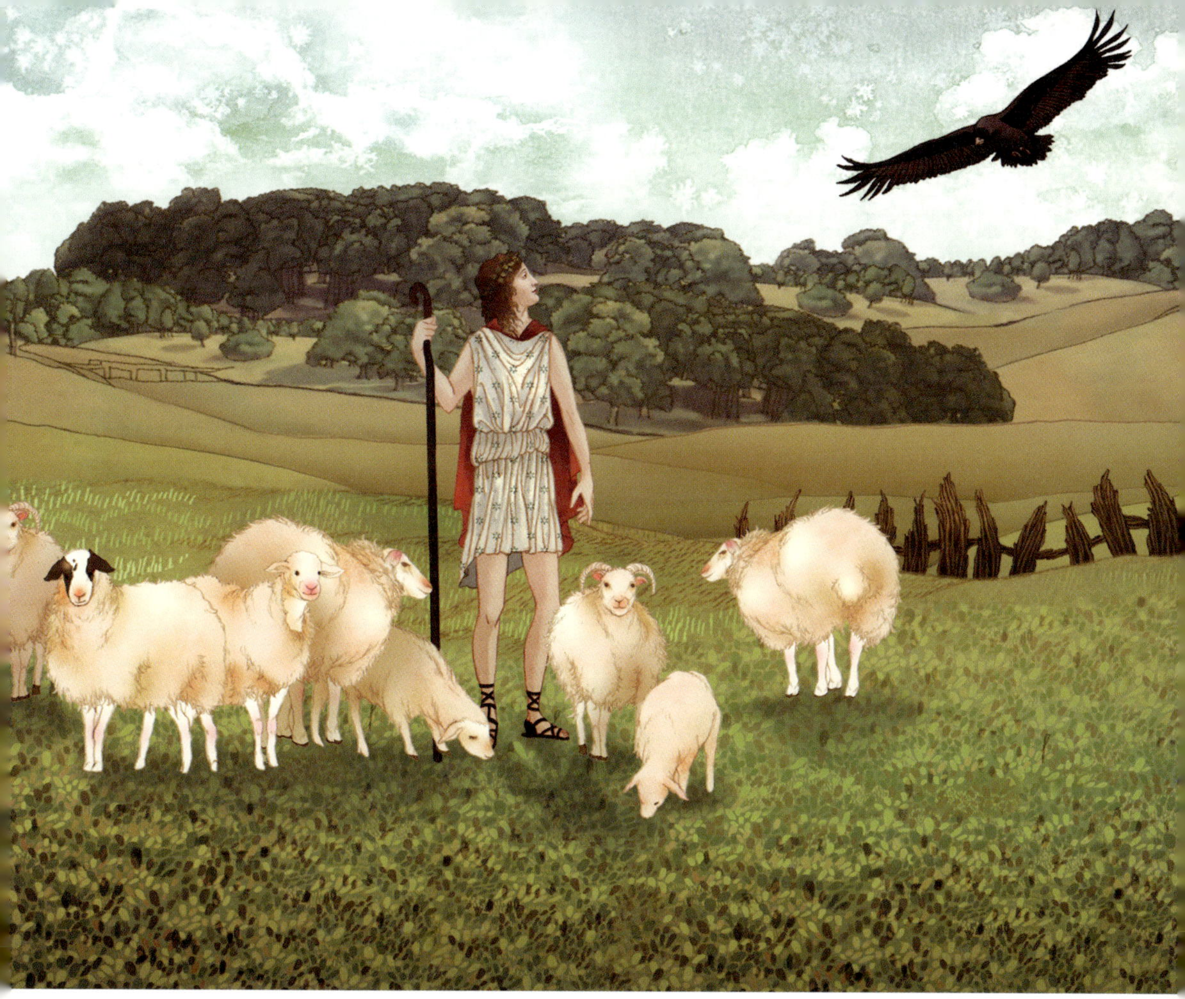

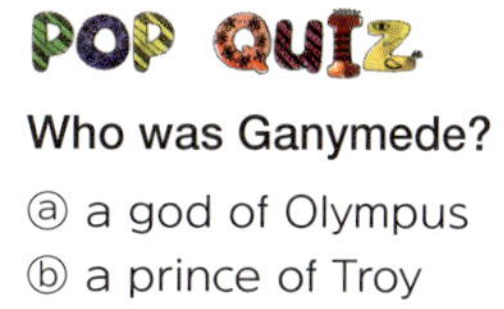

“I don’t know,” Ganymede said. “My father might miss me and what about my life in Troy?”

POP QUIZ

Who was Ganymede?

ⓐ a god of Olympus
ⓑ a prince of Troy

"Become my cup-bearer, and I'll give you eternal youth," 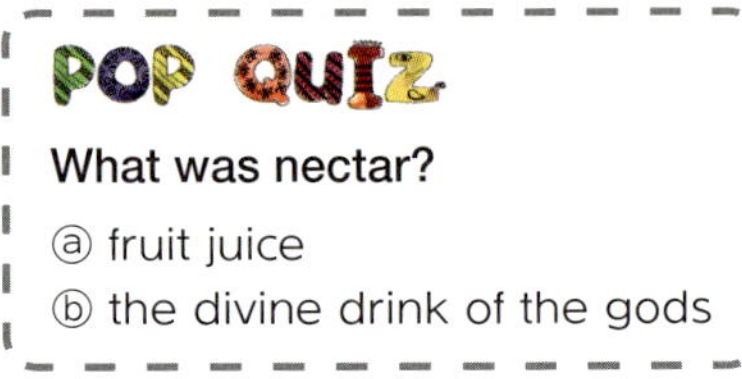
Zeus said. "You will live here with the gods and always look
this handsome. Isn't eternal youth among the gods better
than life in Troy with your father and a herd of sheep?"
Ganymede checked himself out in a mirror hanging near
Zeus. It would be nice to always look this good.
"What is a cup-bearer?" Ganymede asked.
The cup-bearer was responsible for pouring nectar into the
cups of the gods on Olympus. Nectar was the divine drink
that gave the gods their youth and strength.
"Okay, I'll do it," Ganymede agreed.

POP QUIZ

What was nectar?
ⓐ fruit juice
ⓑ the divine drink of the gods

KEY WORDS

- eternal
- youth
- check out
- be responsible for
- nectar
- meal

- entertain
- conversation
- upset
- disappearance
- make up for
- loss

At every meal, Ganymede poured nectar for the gods and entertained them with conversation.

Ganymede made Zeus very happy, but Ganymede's father was upset over the disappearance of his son. To make up for the loss, Zeus sent Ganymede's father two beautiful and fast horses.

Eventually Ganymede died, and Zeus then put him in the sky to honor his personal service.

The stars in Aquarius make the shape of a person pouring water out of a jug. Aquarius is a large and spread-out constellation, but is faint and has few bright stars.

Aquarius can be seen in the fall in the Northern Hemisphere, and in the spring in the Southern Hemisphere. The best time, however, to view Aquarius is at night in the month of October.

This constellation is found near Pisces, Cetus, and Capricornus, which are other water-related constellations. The sun passes in front of the constellation Aquarius between February 16th and March 12th.

KEY WORDS

- personal
- jug
- spread-out

Comprehension Quiz

A Choose all the phrases that describe Pan.

bald head   the form of a human

the horns of a goat   the legs of a goat

no beard   played the violin

B Choose the best answer to each question.

❶ Why was Prometheus being punished by the gods?

   a) He fought against the gods.

   b) He gave fire to humans.

   c) He killed someone.

   d) He helped the Titans in the Titan War.

❷ How did Pan help Zeus after Typhon's attack?

   a) He recovered Zeus's body parts.

   b) He helped Zeus hide from the monster.

   c) He fought Typhon.

   d) He distracted Zeus by playing music.

C Circle the right preposition for each underlined part.

❶ Chiron bravely galloped (<u>into</u> / about) the fray to save his friend.

❷ The centaurs didn't stop shooting arrows (from / <u>at</u>) Hercules.

❸ His arrows had been dipped (<u>in</u> / for) poison.

D Solve the crossword puzzle.

Across ❷ to live forever

❹ Pan _____ Zeus's stolen body parts.

Down ❶ Pan was the god of _____.

❸ Nectar gave the gods their _____ and strength.

❺ What did Zeus send to fetch Ganymede?

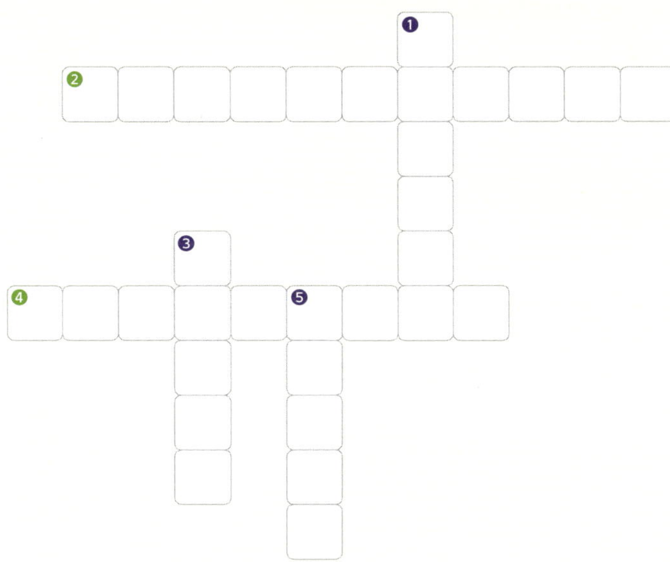

Let's Review the Story

Fill in the blanks to review the story.

Title: ____________

Main Idea: The names of many ____________ are based on Greek and Roman ____________.

Spring Constellations

-Pisces, the ________, represents how ________ disguised herself when ________ came.
-Aries represents the ____ with magical ________ ________.
-Taurus, the ____, represents the ________ that Theseus was able to kill by surprise.

Summer Constellations

-Gemini represents the deep bond between Castor and Pollux, who were ________.
-Leo, the ________, represents the Nemean ________ that Hercules had to kill to fulfill his ________.
-Cancer represents the ________.

Fall Constellations

-Virgo, the young ________, represents Persephone who became Queen of the ________.
-Libra represents the ________ of justice, which belong to Dike, the goddess of ________.
-Scorpius represents the ________ that killed the mighty hunter ________.

Winter Constellations

-Sagittarius represents the ________, who was an ________ and a teacher.
-Capricornus represents Pan, a half-man, ________ creature.
-Aquarius, the ________ bearer, represents Ganymede who Zeus gave eternal ________.

Let's Think & Talk

Think about the following questions and answer them freely.

❶ Looking at the night sky, have you ever seen constellations? Tell us stories you know about the constellations that you have seen.

❷ Tell us what you know about Zeus, King of the Gods in Greek and Roman mythology, and his wife, Hera.

❸ Tell us about the constellations created because of Hercules and the myths related to those constellations.

❹ Which one is your favorite among the Gods, Goddesses and humans in Greek and Roman mythology and why?

Let's Review the Story

Answers

Title: The Myths in the Stars

Main Idea: The names of many constellations are based on Greek and Roman myths.

Spring Constellations

- Pisces, the fish, represents how Aphrodite disguised herself when Typhon came.
- Aries represents the ram with magical golden fleece.
- Taurus, the bull, represents the Minotaur that Theseus was able to kill by surprise.

Summer Constellations

- Gemini represents the deep bond between Castor and Pollux, who were twins.
- Leo, the lion, represents the Nemean Lion that Hercules had to kill to fulfill his labor.
- Cancer represents the crab.

Fall Constellations

- Virgo, the young maiden, represents Persephone who became Queen of the Underworld.
- Libra represents the scales of justice, which belong to Dike, the goddess of justice.
- Scorpius represents the scorpion that killed the mighty hunter Orion.

Winter Constellations

- Sagittarius represents the centaur, who was an archer and a teacher.
- Capricornus represents Pan, a half-man, half-goat creature.
- Aquarius, the water bearer, represents Ganymede who Zeus gave eternal youth.

Smart Readers: **Wise** & **Wide**

After-reading Test

- The Myths in the Stars
- Level 6
- 27 Questions

(Vocabulary 5 / Reading Comprehension 16 /

Sentence Structure & Grammar 6)

1. Which of the following has the closest meaning with the word "reign"?
   ① act
   ② rule
   ③ have
   ④ give

2. Which of the following has the closest meaning with the word "mortal"?
   ① eat
   ② sleep
   ③ die
   ④ live forever

3. Which of the following has the opposite meaning with the word "destroy"?
   ① build
   ② ruin
   ③ devastate
   ④ crush

※ Choose the common word for the two blanks. (4~5)

4.
   - He blew ______ the pipes with all the air in his lungs.
   - The sun passes ______ Libra between October 16 and November 15.

   ① although
   ② throughout
   ③ though
   ④ through

5.

> • How can I ______ my own children whom I love so dearly?
> • Hera chose to honor the lion's ______ by putting it among the stars.

① sacrifice

② satisfy

③ starve

④ stare

6. What did Ino do about her husband's children?
   ① She asked them to leave the kingdom.
   ② She loved them very much.
   ③ She plotted against them.
   ④ She tried to hide them.

7. What did Phrixus do with the golden ram?
   ① He gave it to his father.
   ② He kept it.
   ③ He sacrificed it to the gods.
   ④ He sent it back to Hermes.

8. How should the king and queen of Crete have honored Poseidon?
   ① by throwing a party
   ② by saying a prayer
   ③ through sacrificing the bull
   ④ by taking a swim

9. Why did the king keep the Minotaur?

    ① because the Minotaur scared him

    ② because the Minotaur was his wife's son

    ③ because the Minotaur asked to be kept

    ④ because the king needed to put something in his labyrinth

10. What was Theseus's goal?

    ① to crash the boat

    ② to feed the Minotaur

    ③ to kill the Minotaur

    ④ to save Ariadne

11. What is a centaur?

    ① a Roman warrior

    ② a man who is half-goat

    ③ a creature that is half-man, half-horse

    ④ a creature that is half-bull, half-man

12. How was Hercules punished for killing his family?

    ① He had to perform twelve tasks.

    ② His club was taken away.

    ③ He was rejected by mortals and gods.

    ④ He was whipped by the king.

13. How did Hercules defeat the lion?

   ① clubbed and strangled it

   ② shot it with an arrow

   ③ stabbed it with a knife

   ④ burned it in the cave

14. How did Hercules handle the crab?

   ① He bashed it with his club.

   ② He bit it.

   ③ He stabbed it with his sword.

   ④ He stepped on it.

15. What did Demeter do after Persephone disappeared?

   ① She got angry.

   ② She made flowers grow.

   ③ She attacked the gods.

   ④ She wandered Earth.

16. What makes Libra different from all the other constellations?

   ① It's bigger.

   ② It's brighter.

   ③ It doesn't represent an animal or a person.

   ④ It has the most stars.

17. What do the scales of justice represent today?
　① a constellation
　② a type of clothing
　③ laws which are fair
　④ the absence of war

18. What made Dike leave Earth?
　① greed and war
　② her health
　③ sickness
　④ the beauty of Mount Olympus

19. Who attacked Hercules on the way home from a labor?
　① an Amazon
　② centaurs
　③ a lion
　④ a water serpent

20. What is the first thing Pan did at the beginning of the Titan War when Typhon came?
　① He played his violin.
　② He ran away.
　③ He transformed into a fish.
　④ He warned the gods.

21. What did Zeus offer Ganymede?

   ① all the money in the world

   ② beautiful and fast horses

   ③ a chariot

   ④ eternal youth

※ Choose the wrong part of each sentence. (22~23)

22.
> The bull <u>was</u> <u>much</u> <u>beautiful</u> to <u>destroy</u>.
>   ①   ②   ③   ④

23.
> Hercules <u>had</u> no choice but <u>fight</u> back <u>with</u> his arrows which had been
>   ①   ②   ③
>
> <u>dipped</u> in the Hydra's poison.
> ④

※ Choose the correct word or phrase for each blank. (24~26)

24.
> _______ Ariadne's string, Theseus found his way out of the maze.

   ① Thanks to

   ② Because

   ③ Due

   ④ As

25.
> Eventually Zeus _______ running, turned around, and chose to fight the monster.

① cease
② kept
③ prevented
④ stopped

26.
> He was _______ enormous and strong that he could rip mountains out of the earth to throw them at the gods.

① too
② so
③ such
④ more

27. Choose the correct sentence.

① The people of Nemea can't kill the lion, and can't keeping it from eating them and their cattle.
② The people of Nemea couldn't kills the lion, and couldn't keeps it from eating them and their cattle.
③ The people of Nemea couldn't killed the lion, and couldn't kept it from eating them and their cattle.
④ The people of Nemea couldn't kill the lion, and couldn't keep it from eating them and their cattle.

Brooke Rousseau
Brooke Rousseau is a writer, mother, and French teacher who strives to make the exotic familiar. Driven by a fascination with other cultures, Brooke has lived in Europe, Africa, and the United States, and visited parts of the Middle East and South America. She has earned degrees in French Literature and International Relations. Brooke writes nonfiction for older elementary children, short stories for very young children, and middle grade and young adult novels.

The Myths in the Stars

Retold by Brooke Rousseau
Illustrated by Geumjin Song

First Published in July 2015

Editorial Manager: Juyon Choi
Editors: Juyon Choi, Hyunjung Kim, Kyunghee Jang, Jiyeong Park
Designer: Eunhee Lee
Cover Designer: Eunhee Lee

Published and distributed by

Darakwon Bldg., 64-1 Jandari-ro, Mapo-gu, Seoul, Korea 121-894
Tel: 82-2-736-2031(ext. 250)   Fax: 82-2-732-2037
Homepage: www.ihappyhouse.co.kr
Publisher: Kyudo Chung

ISBN: 978-89-6653-202-5 18740 / 978-89-6653-156-1 18740(set)

[Components]
• 1 Audio CD (Recording Studio: Aram)
• Answer Keys & Korean Translation: Free download at www.ihappyhouse.co.kr